K

DATE DUE

MAY 0 9 2012	
MAY 0 9 2012	
MAY 3 1 2013	
SEP 2 9 2015	
MAY - 7 2018	

BRODART, CO.   Cat. No. 23-221

THE LIFE SCIENCE LIBRARY™

Food and Nutrition

Elizabeth Rose

The Rosen Publishing Group's
PowerKids Press™
New York

For Flannery Emma and Emma Bean

Published in 2006 by The Rosen Publishing Group, Inc.
29 East 21st Street, New York, NY 10010

Copyright © 2006 by The Rosen Publishing Group, Inc.

First Edition

Editors: Rachel O'Connor and Natashya Wilson
Book Design: Albert Hanner

Photo Credits: Cover, pp. 1, 17 © Francesco Ruggeri/Getty Images; p. 5 © LWA-Stephen Welstead/Corbis; p. 7 (top) © Catherine Ledner/Getty Images; p. 7 (middle) © Royalty-Free/Corbis; pp. 7 (bottom right), 9 (bottom right), 15 (bottom), 17 (bottom right), 19 (bottom left) © Photodisc; p. 9 (top) © Dex Images, Inc/Corbis; pp. 10, 19 © Royalty-Free/Corbis; p. 11 (top left) © Ty Allison/Getty Images; p. 11 (top right) © John Kelly/Getty Images; p. 11 (bottom left) © Dennie Cody/Getty Images; p. 13 © David Pollack/Corbis; p. 15 © LWA-Sharie Kennedy/Corbis; p. 19 (top) © Ariel Skelley/Corbis; p. 22 © Stephen Marks/Getty Images.

Library of Congress Cataloging-in-Publication Data

Rose, Elizabeth.
Food and nutrition / Elizabeth Rose.
      v. cm. — (The life science library)
Includes bibliographical references and index.
Contents: You are what you eat — The nutrients you need — Carbohydrates and proteins — Vitamins and minerals — Fat and fiber — Understanding nutrition — Using the food pyramid — The sugar story — Food labels — Healthy living.
ISBN 1-4042-2821-7 (lib. bdg.)
1. Nutrition—Juvenile literature. 2. Food—Juvenile literature. [1. Nutrition. 2. Food habits.] I. Title. II. Life science library (New York, N.Y.)
QP141.R647 2005
613.2—dc22
                                                            2003024797

Manufactured in the United States of America

Contents

You Are What You Eat

Fruits such as oranges are full of vitamin C, which is important for growth. To have a healthy diet, you must know what your body needs. You also need to know which foods are healthy, and which foods are not good for your body.

Have you heard the saying "You are what you eat?" Well, it is true! Your body changes food, such as an apple or a piece of cheese, into **nutrients**. Then your body uses the nutrients for growth, healing, and many other things. Without the nutrients in food, you could not stay alive.

The foods that you eat make up your **diet**. Your diet should be made up of foods that are high in nutrients. Today many people's diets include too much fat and sugar and not enough nutrients. Eating too much fat and sugar can cause heart **disease** and other health problems.

The foods people eat become part of their bodies. That is why it is important to choose a healthy diet, which is good for your body.

5

The Nutrients People Need

People get **energy** by eating food. The measurement used for energy is called a **calorie**. For example, a lettuce leaf has about 5 calories. A hamburger has about 400 calories. People need different amounts of calories every day for a healthy body. Most adults need between 1,600 and 2,200 calories every day. Most children need between 2,000 and 2,500 calories every day to stay healthy. If you take in more calories than your body needs, your body will store the extra calories as fat.

People's diets are different all over the world. However, all people need to eat certain **substances** to stay alive. These six substances are **proteins**, **carbohydrates**, **vitamins**, **minerals**, **fiber**, and fats.

Food is not the only thing people need to stay alive. People also need water. Without water no one can live for more than a few days.

Diets vary around the world. In Asia, for example, the diet consists mostly of rice and vegetables, with some fish and a little meat. It is believed that this plant-based diet guards many Asians from illness.

You do not have to count how many calories you are eating. If you are eating healthy food and getting enough exercise, then you are probably eating what your body needs.

Dairy Fresh

MILK

MILK

Carbohydrates and Proteins

Most of the food you eat is made up of a combination of the six substances. However, we can sort foods into groups by the main substance that makes up each food. Foods such as bread, pasta, rice, **cereal**, and some fruits are made mostly of carbohydrates, or carbs. Carbs provide energy and power for the body. More than half of the energy you need to stay warm and to get through your day comes from carbs.

Proteins are the builders in your body. Fish, meat, cheese, and certain beans all have a lot of protein. Proteins help your body build and heal its cells. They help your body use the energy from carbs. Proteins also help your body **digest** food.

Carbohydrates give you lasting energy for the day. That is why it is so important to eat a good breakfast. These pancakes will give the girl in this picture lots of energy to get her through her long day at school!

Eating proteins and carbohydrates together provides your body with a good balance of the nutrients it needs. It is therefore a good idea to mix carbohydrates with proteins. Peanut butter on bread or a cheese sandwich are great snacks that mix carbs and proteins.
Eating rice with fish or meat makes a good mix, too.

9

Vitamins and Minerals

Iron is a mineral found in red meat, whole-grain cereals, and certain beans. Iron helps red blood cells, shown above, carry oxygen through the body. Oxygen is a gas that has no color, taste, or odor and is necessary for people and animals to breathe.

Human bodies need only small amounts of vitamins and minerals. However, without them, bodies would not work correctly. Vitamins help your body with growth, healing, and other tasks. For example, vitamin A helps your body grow and fight disease. Cheese, fish, and carrots are foods that provide vitamin A. Vitamin C is found in vegetables, oranges, and lemons. It helps form collagen, which is a protein found in bones, teeth, and skin. Minerals are substances your body uses in small amounts to help you grow and keep healthy. Calcium is a mineral your body needs. Calcium is found in milk, cheese, and yogurt.

When your body has a healthy supply of vitamins and minerals, you are able to lead an active and sports-filled life. Vitamins and minerals help make your bones and muscles strong so that you can bike, run, swim, and play soccer!

Fat and Fiber

Wheat is an excellent supply of fiber. It can be found in baked breads, pasta, and cereals. Fiber helps the body digest, or break down, food, and get rid of wastes. To help pass fiber through the body, it is good to drink a lot of water.

Most Americans include too much fat in their diets. Although too much fat is a bad thing, a little fat is good. Like carbs, fat provides your body with energy. Fat is necessary for your body to heal itself. Fat also keeps your body warm in winter. Some fat pads your bones and **organs**, such as the kidneys, to keep them from getting hurt. Fat from plants, such as corn and olives, is healthier than fat from animals. Animal fat is found in meat, eggs, and cheese.

Fiber is a substance that is very important for your body. Fiber comes from plants. It is found in whole-grain bread, cereal, vegetables, and fruits.

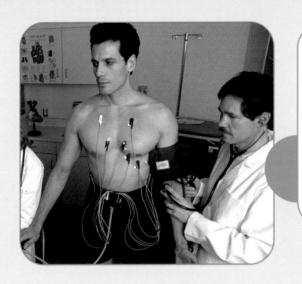

It is very important to keep your heart healthy. One way to do this is to go to a cardiologist to get your heart checked. A cardiologist is a doctor who specializes in treating the heart. A cardiologist will tell you that eating a healthy diet is very important in keeping a healthy heart.

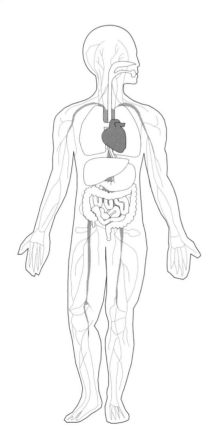

The heart acts like a two-way pump in the body. The left side of the heart receives blood from the lungs and pumps it to the rest of the body. The right side gets blood from the body and pumps it to the lungs. The foods that you eat can affect the health of your heart. For example, if you eat too many foods that are high in fat, like cookies and cakes, the blood vessels in your heart can become blocked. These blockages can lead to heart attacks. Although children do not usually have heart attacks, eating less fat as a child can help you have a healthy heart as an adult.

Understanding Nutrition

The U.S. government has created a food guide to help you make good choices about food. The guide separates food into seven groups. These are fruits, vegetables, grains, meat and beans, milk, oils, and added sugars. The guide offers suggestions on how much you should eat from each group every day. For example, you should eat about five servings each from the fruit and vegetable groups. Fruits are full of vitamins, such as A and C. Vegetables provide vitamins, minerals, proteins, and some carbs. However, you should eat only a small amount from the oils and added sugars groups. If you follow the guide and eat the suggested servings, you will be getting all the nutrients you need for a healthy diet.

The next time you make a trip to the refrigerator, instead of reaching for a slice of cake, choose the healthier option of fruit. Fruits, such as grapes, are full of vitamins and natural sugars that will give you more energy to do the things you love to do.

15

Using the Food Guide

When you look at the guide, it seems like a lot of food to eat in one day. However, a single serving of food may be less food than you think. For example, the guide suggests you eat up to eight servings of grains each day. That does not mean you should eat eight sandwiches! One slice of bread is considered a single serving. If you have two pieces of toast and a bowl of cereal at breakfast, that is three servings from the grain group. If you have a sandwich at lunch, that is two more servings. Popcorn for a snack makes another serving, and one cup of pasta or rice at dinner will give you two more servings. That is eight servings of grains already!

It is important to eat a balanced meal. Next time you go to a restaurant, look carefully at the menu. Check to see if the meals are balanced. For example, do some of the meals include a good mix of vegetables, meat, and grains?

17

The Sugar Story

The food guide recommends that we eat sugar only in small amounts. Why is too much sugar bad for our bodies? Sugar is a carbohydrate, just like pasta or bread. However, pasta and bread are both a kind of carbohydrate called starch. Starch is used up slowly by the body for energy. However, the body burns up the energy in sugar very quickly. This rush of energy, called a sugar high, goes away quickly and leaves the body without any energy at all. If you have a candy bar when you are tired, you might feel energetic for a few minutes. Then you will feel tired again. Sugar also gives the body empty calories, or calories that have no nutrition in them.

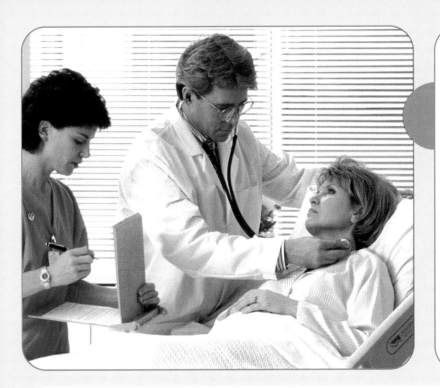

Insulin is an element the body produces to convert, or change, sugars and other food into energy. When the body cannot produce insulin properly, people can become sick with diabetes. The cause of diabetes is not fully known, although overeating and a lack of exercise may increase the chance of getting the illness.

If you need some quick energy, fruit is a better supply of sugar than a serving of chocolate cake! This is because the sugar in fruit comes with nutrients, such as vitamin C. One piece of cake has about .7 oz (19.8 g) of sugar. All that sugar is full of empty calories that will leave you tired. The sugar may get stored by your body as unneeded fat.

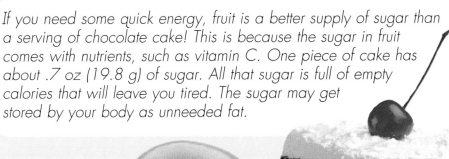

Food Labels

The U.S. government requires that many foods include labels that show the nutrients in the food. You can read these labels to find out which foods are good for you and which are not. The top of the label tells you how many servings are in the food box. One box of food may include more than one serving. The label will tell you how many calories are in each serving of the food. Under calories it will tell you how much fat and sodium, or salt, a serving has. These are things that you do not need a lot of in your diet. Under sodium the label lists proteins and carbohydrates. Toward the bottom it will show you which vitamins and minerals are in the food.

Nutrition Facts

Serving Size 1 Envelope (17g)
Servings Per Container 4

Amount Per Serving

Calories 60   Calories from Fat 10

	% Daily Value*
Total Fat 1g	**2%**
Saturated Fat 0g	**0%**
Cholesterol 0mg	**0%**
Sodium 890mg	**37%**
Total Carbohydrate 12g	**4%**
Dietary Fiber 0g	**0%**
Sugars 3g	
Protein 1g	

Vitamin A 0%	•	Vitamin C 2%
Calcium 0%	•	Iron 0%

*Percent Daily Values (DV) are based on a 2,000 calorie diet. Your daily values may be higher or lower depending on your calorie needs:

	Calories	2,000	2,500
Total Fat	Less than	65g	80g
Sat. Fat	Less than	20g	25g
Cholesterol	Less than	300mg	300mg
Sodium	Less than	2,400mg	2,400mg
Total Carbohydrate		300 g	375g
Dietary Fiber		25g	30g

Calories per gram:
Fat 9 • Carbohydrate 4 • Protein 4

The numbers on the right side of the food label shown here tell you what part of your daily need for that nutrient you will get by eating the food. All foods have different amounts of nutrients in them. Eating foods from all the food groups every day helps you get the right balance of nutrients.

21

Healthy Living

Cigarettes are very harmful to our health. Each year more and more people die from smoking. Smoking can cause heart attacks, lung disease, and many other illnesses. So if someone offers you a cigarette, keep healthy and say no!

Eating right will help you stay healthy. Eating right includes not skipping meals and not eating too much sugar or fat. You can do other things to stay healthy as well. Washing your hands often will help keep you from getting sick from other people's **germs**. Drinking enough water will keep you from feeling tired and getting dried out. Your body heals itself while you sleep, so you need to get 8 to 10 hours of sleep every night. If you eat healthy foods, exercise, drink water, sleep enough, and stay away from harmful substances such as drugs, your body will repay you by growing up to be strong and healthy!

Glossary

calorie (KA-luh-ree) An amount of food that the body uses to keep working.

carbohydrates (kar-boh-HY-drayts) The main elements in foods made mostly from plants, such as potatoes and bread.

cereal (SIR-ee-ul) Food made from grain.

diet (DY-ut) The food a person normally eats.

digest (dy-JEST) To break down food so that the body can use it.

disease (duh-ZEEZ) Illness.

energy (EH-nur-jee) The power to work or act.

fiber (FY-ber) Parts in food from plants that the body cannot break down but that help the body get rid of waste.

germs (JERMZ) Tiny living things that can cause sickness.

minerals (MIN-rulz) Natural elements that are not animals, plants, or other living things.

nutrients (NOO-tree-ints) Things found in food that a living being needs to live and grow.

organs (OR-genz) Parts inside the body that do a job.

proteins (PROH-teenz) Elements inside the cells of plants and animals that help the body grow and heal.

substances (SUB-stans-iz) Matter that takes up space.

vitamins (VY-tuh-minz) Elements in food that help the body fight illness and grow strong.

Index

Web Sites

Due to the changing nature of Internet links, PowerKids Press has developed an online list of Web sites related to the subject of this book. This site is updated regularly. Please use this link to access the list:
www.powerkidslinks.com/lsl/foodnut/